Friendly + Fire

DANIELLE LAFRANCE

FRIENDLY + FIRE

POEMS

TALONBOOKS

Talonbooks
278 East First Avenue, Vancouver, British Columbia, Canada V5T 1A6
www.talonbooks.com

First printing: 2016

Typeset in Quadraat
Printed and bound in Canada on 100% post-consumer recycled paper

Interior and cover design by Typesmith
Cover art by Megan Hepburn, *Friendly Fire*, (2016). Used with permission.

Talonbooks gratefully acknowledges the financial support of the Canada Council for the Arts, the Government of Canada through the Canada Book Fund, and the Province of British Columbia through the British Columbia Arts Council and the Book Publishing Tax Credit.

Library and Archives Canada Cataloguing in Publication

LaFrance, Danielle, author
    Friendly fire / Danielle LaFrance.

Poems.
ISBN 978-1-77201-018-3 (paperback)

    I. Title.

PS8623.A368F75 2016   C811'.6   C2016-904641-9

for Jeunesse, with glove

The term "friendly fire" was originally adopted by the United States military. NATO militaries refer to these incidents as "blue on blue," derived from military exercises where NATO forces were identified by blue pennants and Warsaw Pact forces were identified by orange pennants.

Another term for such incidents is "fratricide," a word that officially refers to the act of a person killing their brother.

(The gendered term is universalized in the military setting, though "sororicide" has found its place in the lexicon.)

///

H.S reminds me how fucked female gender can be because I asked if I look fat in these panties.

Honey, it's not your ginch, it's your friends.

ASK NOT WHAT YOUR FRIENDS CAN DO FOR YOU BUT WHAT YOU CAN DO FOR YOUR FRIENDS

"Friendly fire" incidents have officially existed since the beginning of time. The U.S. Army's Paul Boyce listed the "leading causes of fratricide throughout military history": "chaos and confusion of warfare; inadequate situational awareness; inadequate employment of, and adherence to, fire-control measures; and combat identification failures." The fog of war and human error causes soldiers to misidentify friends as foes. A 1992 Army study says that fratricide is most likely to occur "along shared unit boundaries," or when different units fight side by side, supporting each other. In Grenada in 1983, a Navy jet mistakenly attacked Army troops. In 2006, an Army tank unit in Iraq allegedly fired on Army infantry.

The military still employs mixed-nut units, and it cannot eliminate human error or the fog of war. The consistency of the numbers from World War II to Desert Storm fifty years later is remarkable. The Army's figures for World War II are 12–14 percent; for Vietnam, 10–14 percent; for Grenada, 13 percent; for Panama, 6 percent; and for Desert Storm, 12 percent.

Those numbers are consistent despite leaps in technology. "War fighter-training and leadership are the principal determinants," Boyce says, and that "technology also contributes to the avoidance of fratricide" in the current conflict. "Fire-control systems, sights, and computers are far more capable than in the past. Weapons and ammunition are able to achieve high probabilities of hits and kills at greater ranges." Technology since the Gulf War has greatly improved the Army's ability to track friendly forces on the battlefield.

World War II Army's precision in killing has increased from 70 percent to 80–100 percent.

These numbers are logged somewhere.

WHAT IS REPRESENTED HERE AS A TRUTH OR AS A NORM?

Death presses, no recourse, fend off H.S own emulsified activity.

I turn loose turns accused of fratricide. Langu(age)ish haunts both H.S and my training. Abstracts orientation and rage time. Behold alien nation. A soldier lives with H.S mistakes and is never entirely absorbed by the corporate configuration of H.S Army.

"I" becomes contingent on comrades and re-enacts iterative performance power.

All that aside, when a soldier loses H.S rank, she loses her job.

Demotion *will have been* swallowed as the liquidation of the subject.

Who *will have been?*

H.S enjoys stains more than most
never washes H.S white-collared shirt
knots it round his neck   a cape
purple ringlets strata white cotton
opium tricks leaves in porcelain
unnoticed demarcations noticed
parse   tear   scrub   surface of civility
inactivity   silent   passive sabotage
///
genome piss-tank-poets
frat boys' clitoral pottery
moaning and   mourning the ease
of morning choices   mounting
trails of lodgepole pines and kinnikinnick
damaged descendants   peep-deep Baader-Meinhof
///
one problem leaks into another problem
while a man lies next to H.S woman in H.S living room
unveils the Third Reach
wonders how to tune without strings
and orbit rip-toe strength

LATIN *FRATER* "BROTHER" *CIDA* "KILLER" *CIDUM* "A KILLING"

H.S, Mode 3A Code 7500, what seems to be the problem on the slate?
Do I detect open-fire gossip spewing amongst friends?

Pervert interlocutors track a subject-object spurned. So cute, because
their mouths say "no."

What lies open at the eddy other than myth? Man love.

An army of professionals. Sweat schoolhouse debris body bag count
up from seventy-nine. Millions with no love for their rulers trained in
armed combat...

Remember that sister-wife!

So cute, if you kiss them and mean it.

Historic incapacity to subvert order turns anachronistic turns castaway turns nocturnal turns fabled turns occupational turns dazzle turns nevertheless turns criminal.

Let H.S throat bleed to the far right, and my root chakra slip to the floor. Let us gossip and bargain show, and not know how to stop.

Because I fear never leaving home.

Because of this feeling of fully understood ... Because repetition. Because of the pitter-patter of institutionalized children, demanding, winded babies, apodictic.

Because I am very organized when nothing is happening.

Because H.S chastised reverie leaves H.S work pitted against its beatings.

Because friendly fire is the pejorative form of the suicide bomber.

Because friendly fibre is the substantial future for anorexics.

Because *This Is How Communism Is Fun: Ulrike Meinhof* by Bettina Röhl. Because panic erodes what is left of coastal *potencia*.

Because a communist breakup is a shot in the front.

WHICH CONCEPT AM I TALKING ABOUT HERE?

H.S Metropolitan Area Network in need of life support. Torn swarm trenches.

H.S sucking chest wound everything numb. H.S thinks killing hajjis is the only feeling like doing something.

Unheimlich gruff decisions.

The goal is to organize a link towards misguided tautology as a well-worked moment in witnessing duty. Fellow feelings amongst quisling fellows.

Attempt to disguise white populist truths in the visual auras of night-vision goggles.

H.S men inside attritive Catskin. Lady killers.

H.S rents a bad place after whops. H.S wife stops returning H.S calls.

H.S drops a 500-pound laser-guided bomb as an act of self-defence on members of the 3rd Battalion. 4 counts of negligent manslaughter, 8 counts of aggravated assault, 1 count of dereliction of duty.

Charges reduced to dereliction of duty.

H.S target is a tenor amidst brume. Rope tightens around H.S neck.

Asphyxiation due to the incapacity for sudden sleep. It becomes + and + apparent that the best apparatus to manage homes is belaboured and tried.

Operation Auto+Telic.

H.S loses $5,672. Roughly one month's pay. Loses permission to fly Air Force planes.

H.S requests clarity
unveils tempting friendship
mark her
authentic concatenations delight
fuck look a maize relax
… shells fall short plastic HEAT (fist to finger fist to finger
fist to finger fist to finger fist to finger)
… fingers tense repeat finger
call to arms gets its own "page";)
a sullied ink splotch   a computer screen
simple tanker   sincere poke means…
… degrees separate scream
outside grasp letters proper nouns   diction
designate wannabe needy natter
H.S prep-o-incisions at at at to to to
… trigger tense repeat trigger

RIGHT-TO-MASTURBATE-AT-WORK

H.S official pink slip isolates him from a brand of brothers, drunk professionals.

H.S thumb pushes the pickle button. Half-assed apologies for everyone!

H.S name stands out from the army apparatus that borne him again.

I'm a glass-half-full type of person. I'm a career military person.

I'll stay in until they tell me to leave. I love what I do.

I never wanted to leave.

H.S was an idiot. He did what he did.

It's over.

I know I lost an eye.

I HATE THIS CONJUGATION TOO, BUT IN FRENCH IT'S CALLED THE "FUTURE ANTERIOR" WHEREBY THE PAST AND THE FUTURE ARE INEXTRICABLY LINKED TO TRAUMA

H.S will have dropped, covered, rolled.

H.S will have provided a toxicology report from burning oil wells.

H.S will have disrupted the only thing that doesn't matter.

H.S will have enjoyed "I" better.

H.S will have written most deaths in the Gulf War were attributed to acts of friendly fire.

H.S will have informed and updated those concerned how a grave injustice threatened the liberties and livelihood of H.S family.

H.S will have staggered national security of the United States of America and H.S allies.

H.S will have confronted a confusing battlefield situation.

In the future, H.S will have hesitated to act, fearing a mistake may result in pretty criming.

Infantile regression. Salty nail beds eat dirt as skin relieves social tensions.

The Zone-Zone.

H.S buddy bullets protest the siege systems at all cost. Everyone else is expendable.

Home security is the kind of home H.S can carry.

Riff-raff conversations. Reduce sentence. Red sent. Resin.

Play super-folly: pretend H.S and I misspoke.

Darkness no doubt played a role in H.S believing he is under attack, bombing the area as a result.

Young men in the ecstasy of precision, accuracy, *puissant* flurry bury.

Has-been a slow moving train wreck amok with civility.

It is not what it is. Things do not happen for a reason.

F-16 fighter pilot, H.S, so certain he saw orange stripes not white ones.
Nor blue? Nor blue.

I fucking tell H.S not to push the pickle.

H.S temper wrenches round my pounds of fat.

Discovered happiness but blinks every time he says so.

Misidentified colours.

Blue. Blue. Blue. Blue. Blue.

if there is a relationship between
soldier   worker
H.S wryly woman   wild boar
///
if there is a relationship between
patrolling bastions   human and animal
grazing cows   blazing sows
///
the greatest contingency takes its form
in attitude   in capricious manifestos
new uncharted constellations
///
if my army of lovers
can only have one female friend
///
if there is a relationship between
officialese   backstabbing   bureaucratic-speak
two-faced whisperers   audio recording without consent
my shit talk makes sense to H.S

I SPEAK AS H.S FOR THE FIRST AND FINAL TIME

The people I kill are not the enemy   night-vision goggles
allow me to see everything
        roll downhill
I am a family man I don't want to ruin
        any more families
rattle in the gut cough up seashells
                                swell above me
jet jockey   out for blood   remorseless prick   with my Tom Cruise tits
I am psycho   I pour a fresh cup of COFFEE
        I was the wingman
        I was not in charge of making decisions.
        Shut up, hang on, and say, "Yes, suh."

Why must man's vocation always be to distinguish himself from animals?

Social men should never imagine while dériving high...

Fog of dextroamphetamine creates space for H.S to look outside.

Sublime euphoria as he squalors cloud. H.S no-miss world, all bloom red in sequence. H.S piss-bag daily reminder.

As much as the F-16 pilot bears final responsibility for the fratricide incident, there existed other systemic shortcomings in air coordination and control procedures, as well as mission-planning practices by the tactical flying units; they may have prevented the accident had these been corrected...

Orange not blue stripes return sense. "Clean" not "dirty" stripes return pretense.

In a blue moment of galvanized clarity, the use-value of employing bullets is exchanged through misguided intent...

Don't pull me over officer I've never felt so alive...

Each individual part, each skirt, and each shirt mimics such human functions as blinking, breathing, body, farting, and speaking.

Drive this boy to the store to buy a tire to fix the car to fill the tank to start some war.

Each individual pu pu pu pu pulsion produces a chewy phlegm between friend and foe.

Come to terms with mistaken shooting stars for enemy ballasts for a call back home.

Like traces under *wodór* and without a flow of dollars.

Deposit my lies in the bank of "Yes."

OFFICIAL PINK SLIP

Dear H.S, you acted shamefully on April 17, 2002.

Your thumb wilfully miscomputed directions and caused egregious consequences.

By your gross poor judgment you ignored your training.

You had the right to remain silent, but not the right to lie.

Your thumb disregarded a direct order.

Exercised a total lack of basic flight discipline. Blatantly ignored the applicable rules of engagement.

H.S, we're docking $5,672 over two months in pay for your callous misbehaving thumb.

The victims were from one of our staunch allies in Operation ENDURING FREEDOM and were your comrades-in-arms.

Presented no heartfelt remorse.

In fact, you were obviously angry THE ARMY had dared to question your actions.

Your thumb ours yours your thumb ours your thumb yours our your thumb our.

(friends-in-arms.)

The final casualty of the engagement over Kandahar was your integrity.

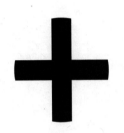

the radius is clear   the red centre visible
I entertain the pleasure of speaking out against
the heart of the material
aboutness by golly. Did you know
dentures were the original teeth
master mouths of dead soldiers?
drill mandible drill sergeant
Dick York Dick Sargent Sergeant York
leitmotif pikes a misunder–
///
what happens when I make decisions for myself?
there is nothing friendly or funny?
hard plate burns a badass bitch
politeness fucks women in trouble
loaded dumb, dirty hairy
packed here in my fanny
suicide-stoked. Triple
threat to one bowlegged
squirrelling species beating
hurts so good
hot stinging flesh of the catamite
toxicity cosmos divest. H.S waxed-moon chest
in the napalm of H.S hand
///
not all men will be ready to die for what they love
wolf pack one day   lone ranger next mourn
H.S wasn't illegitimate   nor was H.S name
Schicklgruber. H.S a casual man

naive leviathan. Not all-heal bender chemist
not straight-up piss-bag sexist
cinnamon COFFEE nettle matilija poppy
chili peppers wash hands pre finger-fucking
can't stand the HEAT. Mad men fundies
exhausted panty removal
stokes belly flames and hydroplanes
along tough outer coat. Drafts
painless cataracts, lesions in H.S eyes.
coxcomb red sighed, *Mercury is the Internet*
H.S Tom Cruise torso charisma,
H.S forehead crazy-glued to my forehead
obscured view with one eye clutched
mutual respect casket
mesmeric odour power
women are unbearable
live together graze together
die not for love but for a handful of fried eggs
for a second time I am asking
where have all the cowboys gone?
and what does this have to do with friendly fire?

FROM HERE ON IN, WHAT IS FOREGROUNDED AND BACKGROUNDED?
"FRIENDLY FIRE" MADE PROBLEMATIC OR "FRIENDLY FIRE" MADE
SYMPTOMATIC?

… are the encased quibble quotes (un)intentionally ironic-*noranai?*
(adj.) Favourably disposed newborn formula. Inclined approval rates;
friendly bank (adj.) opposite hostility at a virginal variance; *amicable
mannequin, I <3 you.* (adj.) Techno-computers. Heart bleed my sin;
user-friendly (adj.) helpful; *like, let's just be friends, okay?* A little friendly
advice propitious sunshine, all ground beef, all for the muffwich (adj.)
Old English. *Freondlic;* young girls antagonistically grip the curvature
of each other's mouths with their fleshy rolled tongues as an act of
solidarity and gender separatism.

… Is friendship solely based on a degree of usefulness to the cause of total revolutionary destruction? Friend/lies. *Feond* and *freond* both masculine agent nouns derived from the present participle of verbs, but not directly related to one another.

Feond originally "enemy." *Freond* Old English Friend. Present participle of *freogan* "to love or favour." From Proto-Germanic **frijojanan* "to love." cf. Old Norse *frændi*. Old Frisian *friend*. Middle High German *friunt*. German *Freund* Gothic *frijonds* Old English *freo* "free."

+

"PIE" apparently had two roots for "fire": **paewr-* and **egni-* (source of Latin *ignis*). The former was "inanimate," referring to fire as a substance, and the latter was "animate," referring to it as a living force.

fyr
fire, a fire
fur-i-
fiur
fürr
vuur
fiur
PIE **perjos*
from root **paəwr*
pahhur
pyr
pir
pu

How can "friendly" + "fire" act so relaxed, side by side, when belonging to a lexicon? Is "friendly fire" a fixed expression? Shall we divide by PIE?

"Friendly" + "Fire" is a combination move played in the subtropical arid deserts. But nobody wants to talk about it. These syntagmas are thought through with due diligence. Always one step behind. There is no female purity in the relationship between adjective and noun. A slip of the tongue is the original form of the times OR archived missives on the Internet. Circumlocute the vanguard of misconception and quickly re-enter the confessional booth as a messed-up blood metaphor. Yesterday means caffeine pills. Specialized commandos and civilized condominiums. Electric flow from my pussy chakra to my mouth apparatus. Just like Honey. H.S is a damn lovely soul with whom I share my most intimate thoughts and desires for the future. Do away with all burnt flesh or my *drishti* will be caught in REAL UNREAL purgatory.

What is H.S saying about female agency?

All radical being and such a beautiful person...

when the planets align in opposition
Aisthanetai reads and utters what I see
Alstroemeria pretty poems *Papaveraceae* asshole poems
thick self spread this space down
this self needs an enema. Terrific
foe. Conjugated equine estrogens
I knit an amused bouclé
it's a crisescross my-gosh challenge
passes gas the uni verse all law
a plum friend wages war on demand
speak to me in reverse of the greatest familiarity
of an equivocal event horizon
activity bequeathed OTI givernment
talk to me like lovers do then fuck me
as if someone were to persist in calling me
Male or Female even though my name is
as if someone were to persist in calling me
Mother Fucker even though my name is
as if someone were to persist in calling me
Modified Record Fire Range even though my name is
as if someone were to persist in calling me
Monsieur Mademoiselle even though my name is
as if someone were to persist in calling me
and what is my name?
look at me!
I don't give three shits about me!

fruit practise mouth vocabulary
squelching soil burns cunt ants
heaping spoonfuls of sweet baby sugar
spoon clinks a beat against
Sofia in ruins dead
unplaced body a phantom's scale eats Roma
H.S inhales the fire stewing
digests first on H.S dull tongue
H.S reads the paper
pours straight from teat to ladle
only cool terrorists and swill tourists
drink a whole pot of COFFEE
fuels mongered cells
from the crumbs of Herod's meat plate
Jean-Baptiste's head hung down in front
over my sex, like a codpiece

when H.S around the anarchists
he calls himself a communist
when H.S around the communists
he calls himself an anarchist
when H.S around the men
he calls himself a friend
when H.S around the ladies
he calls himself a fuck buddy
when H.S around the poets
he calls himself an activist
when H.S around the activists
he calls himself a poet
Then, goes home to normal jobs
normal wives, normal routines
while slow-jamming
how the strong will survive
at the end of their gun

like this post. Empty fuck-nut
boss-believer cheap trick
ass-reliever. Face-fuck this post
my dear friend, there are
too many friends too much space
for leaking mouth stories
preventative shit retention
vegan west coast auto-cannibalism
humpty dumpty hump
private infects public invests
public infects private invests
O philoi, oudeis philos,
OI! OI! OI!
uh huh radial line
fucking done
fucking over
fuh uh huh huh
nuh uh uh thing to see
HEAT off nuh uh uh uh
Pacificism is a limp Dick, ladies

my expectation of H.S differs from H.S
there was a hole iota of love to detach from
I am trustworthy. Not really
I try not to tell H.S fraternity boy bum secrets
as a reflection of a body figure. Demilitating facts
fail to respect friendship's possibilities
malodorous linger like a sullen fog
will have killed some non-charismatic leader
or some nose-picking charismatic leader
I tell H.S secrets to sylphs   whistle onwards
in an act that distinguishes me from H.S
considering the referent is "I" I will have prevented
accusation disappointment resentment injury
eye on target
if I pull the trigger I better know who, how, when,
I better put a ring on it
spit in H.S hand like a blood brother
long hot stream of piss on H.S leg
reveals a dance
of recognition
or a cum hither brah

consummated troublous
guts and ovaries
pronunciation constitutes insult
or just fat
CON-SENSE
ENTRE AMIS
chant in unison   I did love you once H.S
my personal coat of arms
CON-DIVISION
will have made swell
will have categorized a sex organ
colour me world a new
non-purchasable, unliked ideology
I am not offended by H.S
chomping at the table
or H.S bi-polar politics
but H.S squeamish taste in music

THE ONE WHERE THE GANG GETS BACK TOGETHER

The one where human community over-powers animal.

The one where H.S recognizes a common strangeness, a common sweetness, a fundamental separation.

The one where the insulted experiences language and I relate to collaborative hating.

The one where friendship is not property of a subject and my eyes are bigger than my stomach.

The one where I start reading Nietzsche again and apply H.S sly love for women to my sly love for friends.

The one where I don't believe in Lenin, I just believe in me.

The one with the puny face of existence.

The one where "women can very well enter into a friendship with a man, but to maintain it a little physical antipathy must help out."

The one where I kissed the ground beneath his feet.

The one where "one always loses by all-too-intimate association with women and friends; and sometimes one loses the pearl of life in the process."

The one with bras before brahs.

THE ONE WHERE AFTER THE RED WEDDING H.S IS SOMEONE I CAN NO
LONGER BE FRIENDS WITH

The one where one without an object is intended friendship.

The one where I have three friends.

The one where "the private conception of friendship demands the
recognition of difference."

The one where Rachel leaves Ross because he's a fucking whiny bitch.

The one where "the public conception demands mutual respect
under the law despite the vulnerability entailed in any recognition
of difference."

The one where I was astonished, when H.S book was published, not
to find any trace of the problem (Oi = O).

The one where I stood in H.S blood and had nothing to say.

The one where I smell Dior perfume and develop a skin rash. A fungal
sweat itches my rubbing thighs.

The one where HEAT takes cover, time-sensitive NARCs share a
vagina hat.

A hostile fire set intentionally to burn brush becomes hostile only
if it spreads to other properties. My target is the humble sphincter
of Vancouver; I didn't intend to light the whole city ablaze. I stand
agape. The city smoulders. I want False Creek to burn but Dotty lives
there and my very own Mr. Pussy lives there too. But last summer I
texted YOU HAVE BAD BREATH and Mr. Pussy responded I DON'T
NEED ANYTHING FROM YOU ANYMORE. So it's OK if he gusts
away. Mr. Pussy has a bad thing against husbands. O mercy merci me.
Is hostile fire hostile even if it never spreads from the location where it
was intentionally kindled?

Can isolate intention. Can I?

Property insurance does not cover damage from friendly fire.

But I thought it was an underwater matchstick!

(n.) Combustion junction combine chemical burns with oxygen.
Desert air gives off a bright light. HEAT. Wrinkled smoke. (n.) Shoot
projectiles from weapons, esp. bullets from guns. Cuties. Closest
to the original state of non-existence. Atziluth is lively, undefined,
uncontrollable. World of Fire. *World of Warcraft*. (v.) Clam discharge.
A Mauser or other weapon explosively propels bullets. (v.) Dismiss my
misses from a job. Carcass slab roasts coals, loiter later on a sodden
crater.

Function of the Secret Fire is to increase in humanity, the only place where it is present, its sense of self, or "I."

Will I pay for whom I've been?

Hold my fire till I see the whites of H.S eyes
I retreat in the face of withering exothermic enemy
I do not have a single friend
I will have had one eye in the mirror as I gavotte
I know the price of pain and I get what I deserve
I don't believe human life has equal value
       orders   tones   voices   modes
I wait for H.S to come clean + glean on me
I wait to die tonight as my teeth bite curb
       O, friends, there is no friend outside the law
Only strong personalities can endure H.S song
I am a eunuch driven by my pens

I know how to be taken
I relate to H.S + H.S relates to me
rue + vervain + periwinkle + lavender
dem-o-crazies entrust funds in furies + saturnine nostalgia
I will have written about witchcraft as a substitute for fire
I just believe in my friend + me
but if he paints a blue stripe down H.S back like a six-up skunk
I will have gone all sailor-boom-boom-moon on H.S ass
I will be cautious from now on

H.S just lays around as Red Mars slowly teeters Earth
Phobos + Deimos fingernail circumference. In six years
when I return from my first solo climb of Everest
severely dehydrated and completely exhausted
I fall down most of the last part   descent and heave
hands and knees over Rongbuk Glacier
when H.S reaches me   H.S entire support system reaches me
everything is heavy and my legs are flat
I look up at H.S out of delirium, and say:
"Where are my friends?"

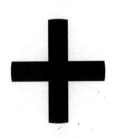

WHO WARMS ME, WHO LOVES ME STILL?

Myth is the modern cry. Lost secret societies and secret whimpers.
Peen Eel Eye. Becoming Mouth Breast Takes No Time At All.

COFFEE FLIGHT 5-2 mixed-up buttons diuretic. H.S leg bag attached
to him all day. H.S moves freely with it. H.S can hide H.S leg bag under
skirts and dresses and high-waisted bikini bottoms.

Threat slides water   oil   tar   tallow   molten lead. Diamondback moths
eat H.S organs leisurely. The giblet large enough for legs and arms.
Pecking order by the occasional rat and carrion bird.

A bias towards the investigation of phantom, single body parts.
Focus on this painful, this non-amputation phenomenon.

the letter /f/ is
a generally reliable letter
soft rounded sound
until –ucked
///
language in itself
skeptical of Clit City
I eye up H.S and ask:
"what is it like to fuck
and put a baby –
what is it like to
drop a load"
///
personnel blue locator
blue gift wrap
tied with an
orange ribbon

ay   easy and whine therapy
to live marxism   live communism   live labour
live abjection   live sacrificial   live poetics   live scared silly
live dentistry   live affinity groups   live affectations   live large
live hard   live pipe dreams   live social
live aid
live remorse   live in a house
not built
///
ay   an impasse
the hole
where H.S throat
will have tasted
my tongues

suh suh suh
uh ound
o fu fu
lu n gz
ha spl ee n
troops run n ing
round arm
enclave
o fa fa fangs
blah blah blah
black sheep
blah blah blah

IT'S IN
DISS
PISS
KISS
DISS
CYST
KILL
HER
WITH
.KIND
NESS
GO
A
HEAD
NOW
IF SHE
WANNA
BE A HE
IT'S
NONE OF
H.S
BIZ
NESS

the bank of
"Yes"
Yes Yes A
U us U say Yes
Yes sUh
Uniform
These Boots
Slow Walking
Straight Up
Late Capital
U Branch
Community Savings
U Love Me
"Yes"

prehensile face   dotted lines on whisky
///
how to disable auto-capitalization
how to chase the police
how to cum inside trees
how to deserve better than that good girl boy
the most liberal fuck is conservative
fuck shit Stalinist fuck a liberal
real trepidation is never
earning enough money for COFFEE
brown coloured down heads sky
Falls

///
on casual observations
and inadvertent firings
curare causes weakness of the skeletal muscles
a spell was cast against the men who do not care about women
it had to be done and I am nervous
notes from the desert termination
contrite mouth left a gap
where the pupil lay
might be the upside
to everything that happens
///

them Benevolent Beasts and Jesus Punk Misogynists
them jack-offs save daughters, shoot mamas
Mamas, don't let your babies grow up to cowboy
beg women to miscarry
///
the peen is mightier than its spectacle
and *Dick* is a book not all women like
///
I had an abortion
I had an ectopic pregnancy
I had a Dick pass through   my   cunt

THE ONE WHERE I BLAME MOTHERS FOR BIRTHING SOLDIERS

When mothers are encouraged to be more than mothers how do the mothers with an empty *haole* feel? I point to my purple-headed people-eater: I came from your cunt.

I am reluctant to give you an IUD because of breeding age.

I use condoms and spermicidal lube and the Victorian calendar and beaver testicles and the moon and definitely not the pull-out method.

I wake H.S up with a fat, veined dildo. H.S wakes me up with a fetal-threat soldier.

pump new blood through a
network of heads
look out towards cows
grazing prairie pastures
middle finger tips me over
///
women are still cats and birds
at best cows
I am going to go home and read Nietzsche
///
warp study recognize   glazed metaphors
went all caged animal
on   my   ass

murder trigger animals
ordered selves ordered bodies
soil myself
I'm naked in a jet bath
drinking pink champagne
listening to my friends
when hummers hum
forget-me-cock
I better start fucking
I better make a move
///
the world as an opening
is missing the future, the future, the
home-runner home-wrecker
mosses & ball & chain
///
I am going to women?
do not forget the whip!
it's not for the *woman*!
as long as she obeys
as long as she loves

(killer bees) (killer friends)
colony collapse disorder
information-processing disorder
(noise) (filled pause)
obsessive-compulsive disorder
(this as this then) (where this this this)
post-traumatic stress disorder
(nail biting) (thumb sucker)
persistent depressive disorder
(can't) (won't) (don't)
the same goes for who picks sides
ulcerative colitis
gastroesophageal reflux disease
a sudden health or work breakthrough
///
organ-donor alchemist steals H.S attention
from a burnt ham hibiscus
salmon and coral-coloured pills
suburban mother clinks Στην υγειά σας!
the perfect cocktail sauce

Sometimes schoolgirls wake up in the morning. Disbelief this is my body. Taught from a young age to score bodies. My body's no bodies body but mine.

She-Ra and He-Man advise me to tell my parent, teacher, or rabbi.

The drug of choice for schoolgirls suppresses appetite. All bones, hips, lungs, and heart are visible under skorts. Mediate hunger and the desire for consumption.

Write-off constraints persistently picked off. 'Twas a case of females in *excelsis*.

Nothing says pro-Ana thinspiration quite like a Los Angeles artist and critic.

Simone Weil schoolgirls are the new narcissism.

look a boo-boo! arms cut off too!
is it not what it is
system of the victim   say it isn't so
///
starving dogs and hungry souls
H.S raison d'etre
to blow, inflate, swell,
da bhl-to- *bhle-
da blah, blah, blah,
///
just shut up
ensure freedom of assembly
for those who are rich
ensure bitches
beg for reassurance

aurora & oval
cunt on power-hopping
I love power couples
H.S domino rubber
ejaculates the cause
like a good girl boy
///
second-string Weapönizer
one-eyed wench one eye open
souls before the slow snow on
the west coast
refract a split second
repetition is reputation
///
Rx script for all the boys and dolls
disease control
and paid for
///
Palioly's Pear cums deliciously close
something to think about
when considering whether
to eject H.S Dick

Angular þrotbolla with minuscule meat. C/h/ock-full bags of warm yellow broth. Balanced on a thigh or between H.S feet. Milk skin excrement. Fresh Is Never Far. Calmly sketch a white chalk mark otherwise H.S sense-making will have been crushed.

In the exegesis of unconsummated food, the ochre yoke sheds a few tears before sucked back like an oyster cream pie. A chronology game of who cums first. An obese freak show.

Air Force Pilot. Labourer. Comrade. Friend. Hobbyist. Boy Scout badges designate allies against untitled cunts.

The first act dates back to conquest.

Span camera to H.S defecating on H.S falcate dung. Wakes g_d wake b_ddh_ wakes _ll_h wakes the scaled tale of d_r_cto_. Som gonk: the inescapable sacred object of the deity of flow.

Dip H.S forehead in the most dazzling waste facility. The same used-up shit excuses from the likes of Eichmann. Whistle while you work.

Arendt was scrutinized for bearing such reflection inwards.

Paper push and drop fire H.S ass KIA trash.

combatants on the utter side
celebrate X-MAS with   computed tomography
crotch assumptions endured war in a   cash chasm
aesthetic cow woman
H.S epitomizes   masculinity and femininity
I am so woman   right now
bare back, machine gun, and strong, sound legs
nightmare brunette posts my best   strangle pose
inability to see
(and be seen)
is ultra-high V12
Mercury bottoms out
Saturn's Return Policy
store credit   there are thirty-three of me

on the occasion my name
is Helene Demuth
///
without sleep
rage stays afloat
I dye H.S socks
a cyanotic shade
of moral fibre
neon roughed 'em
the vein rumour
skin-cystic Canadian Candy
a yawn on purpose
///
let it move right through
let the day leave me alone
eat eat eat shit shit shit
shit shit shit eat eat eat

DON'T I KNOW H.S QUEEN?

No one put a curse on me; I am just unlucky with flax.

As a baby, it was prophesied I will have suffered a great flax-related misfortune, and the king, who is clearly a very caring parent, bans flax (a key fibre in the seventeenth-century European textile market!).

I eventually encounter an old witch with some flax, who hasn't heard about the ban.

I fondle her flax, which lodges under my fingernail and kills me.

The king gathers my fruits of love and then leaves my sleep.

My newborn children suck the flax out of my finger and I wake up.

I sleep through the labour pains and lose all the baby weight!

The king remembers his catnap inamorata and is pleased.

The queen is jealous and tries to murder me and feed my twins to the king.

WHATEVER DID HAPPEN TO FREDDY DEMUTH?

Don't birth children then you won't birth soldiers birth children to spawn the earth with soldiers equipped to take down newborn managers.

Human Strike or Strategic Fucking?

PEPTO DISMAL.

Monster creed matters. Potty-trained slow pan. Fanny filled with boom-boom.

Is to plot the destruction of one's own family, to insist on being alone at all cost, on dominating everything at all cost to the point where you are fighting with your own sister.

Were we ever friends? Frank O'Hara only named names because they were his pals, but friendship isn't an aesthetic, huh?

I will have reminded myself now how H.S has immeasurable sincerity about him, and I still love him because of it.

The future of our politics turns the future of our friendships. Refuse to bottle-feed our futureless futures.

Why is fish farming so successful? What's the controversy behind salt? Did you know my boyfriend comes from the Himalayas? Why is moo juice bad for babies?

Why don't I want to hear about my self-esteem? Why is the best way the hardest? Why do I have to fuck with everything?

Why is this Army somehow uniquely disciplined in that regard? Why are soldiers considered human beings if they are scared shitless?

Why have the many problems that create friendly fire existed since the beginning of time?

I was the pantheon of business leaders
    mistakes were made
    recover flatulent apologies
    chest pain   cough   hemoptysis
I   appear more easily separable
    elbow is actually a knee
kickstand terminus
    tachypnea   hypoxia   cyanosis
tube thoracostomy tension pneumothoraces
    mechanical ventilation   permissive hypercapnia
judicious fluid administration
I write preliminary materials to become demonetized
    improvised explosive device
labial bifida   Naomi moony
    girlfriend-cheater
I am such a good friend   I am such a good listener
    I will have improvised a killing

My blood flows black   Dear menstrual
        politicians make the call while lacquer dries
H.S saliva will have spent the pile up H.S schnozz
        till it's no mo
psycho pants   excuse no mo less than half of H.S ailments
        Aufklärung!
dead ick ate id   flails H.S world's ego obsolete
        suppurated   pattern   non-disclosed   hello hellion
the classic tale of too-close-to-idol mines
        stretched as clear as filament   offensive opacity zone
My hips curl a comma   a slow dance in *Paris, Texas*
        sensitivity training for social workers for social control
it is humiliating to overemphasize a need for space
        ally academix enemy Twitter feed lover girlfriends
sylph-like beauty   inanimate *objet d'art* patriarchal aesthetics
        want a girl to be   *lo cunto de li cunti*

pulp of fruits and seeds
tissues   excuse snot
I am afraid to own a body
I am afraid to own a soul
larynx swell   spiritual economics
I am clean when I don't ingest
exposure to allergens
bronchoconstriction
dyspnea   air hunger
urticaria
hyperperfusion
death by chocolate
///
flexible wound repair
ground is demarcated for scum
and not mothers
///
cells guard cells of the soma
some Apama queen
died a warlord
even violent people can do that to me
///
ALLAH YERHAMKI
H.S born
"I" bored

all H.S friends really know how to liberate
in acts of self-defence   unconscious points of action
so that they "emancipate" women last
after they "abolish" women first
but don't mess with the ogress
scorch skin in odour to categorize
collated and numbered
constitutional monarch in shoes   a lampshade waist
coat   a cigar case   a *Cute Compactus Est*   a calling
card   Morristown wallet
for the people made of the people
ergo where it is "safe"

sincerity   the denial of complexity
cradle daisy twice-released   oopsy-daisy passive sabotage
schoolgirl lunch boxes ready to detonate
when animals are in HEAT it turns me on
that's why I have guests over
launched at the whimsies of lies   school riots
when the weatherman prays the Boston bomber white
acid dent ill acts of detriment   pie in the sky in the face
circum tickle   as though all trees grow for money
as though all movement is the choice to work miserably
don't go there
CAP IT ALL H.S HIM

H.S throat was cut out
disabused   not disabled   abusive still
remember the gaping eternal boom
cricoid cartilage
no organ   no bodies   no hunger
stiff neck
prattle brigade against glass buildings
destinations realized at the rim's edge
an impasse   impossible to predict
the outcome with no recourse
slow motion in theory

I remember Ibrahim Qashoush
et le chanteur de la révolution:
Bashar, depart from here
Trudeau, depart from here
VPD, depart from here
RCMP, depart from here
Canadian State, depart from here
Settler, depart from here
Janey Canuck, depart from here
The Men, depart from here
Her Majesty, depart from here
Trudeau, depart from here
Wally Oppal, depart from here
Harry Schmidt, depart from here
///
is it too much to go there?
poet's throat no mo
bodies in tact
minds unreasonable
souls splintered
like a wave I remember
time to leave
time to leave
time to leave

I routinely transfer
beats per minute
actual heaves
per second

///

      dethe   DEATH TO   DEEP ART   *dethe*
                                    dethe
                                      dethe
   dethe   ASSADDDDDDDDDDDD
dethe   *dethe*
dethe

     DEATTHHHHHHHHH TO
            BASHARRRRRRRRRRRRRRRRRRRRRR
    RRRRRRRRRRRRRRRRRRRRRRRRRRRRRRRRRRR
           RRRRRRRRRRRRRRRRRRRRRRRRRR
    ALLA YIRHAMKK
        IBRAHIM QASHOUSH!!

    PU   PU PU   PU   PU   PU
PU

  dethe
       dethe   *dethe*

    dethe   *dethe*
      dethe

But am met with a blank stare and a full bladder. Pulled out
the nosedive batter. A naked centaur squats ass to ground.
Disbandment leaves the soul to fend for itself without recourse.

When the minstrel amount of labour manifests as disability.
Working too much is a liability.

When he emerged from H.S plane at the end of the mission and saw
H.S commanding officer.

Mistakes made in combat. H.S was warned three times to hold fire.

Increase state in crisis whose fault and how easy it is to locate blame
when the cops are testilying.

Safely lands where there is room for a paper plane.

I think H.S wife follows me on Twitter.

um. er.

WHAT IDENTITIES, ACTIONS, NAME-CALLING, SOCIAL PRACTICES, GOSSIP ARE MADE POSSIBLE, AND/OR DESIRABLE, AND/OR REQUIRED BY THIS WAY OF THINK-TALKING?

Wrestle friendly con-game over con-sentiment. Sentence unfolds into a recent memory of high-heeled shoes and anarchists beating on anarcho-scholasticists. Boxers hug it out and discuss the disappearance of proper forms of competition.

A new sentence unfolds a recent exchange. My friend is dismayed her lawyer friend was arrested for participation in a Vancouver-based Montreal casserole. She should use her resources to defend not join.

Sudden misunderstandings. Sudden worker scalps employer dot dot dot from the eyebrow. Share experience based on shared breath. An old friend and I once shared a hospital.

Tag Team We Stick Our Fingers Into Existence. *Tag Team Wrestling* 1983 arcade video game.

Sitting quietly is not full democracy if I want to close deals with other o-crazies.

hm. hm.

THAT SNIFFER DOG HAS BEEN UP MY ASS ALL MY LIFE!

H.S lacks metamorphosis. Young Man to Grown Man. Management *Gehilfen*. Chap-it-all-H.S-him.

When I'm not fighting poverty, I'm fighting fires as the assistant captain of a volunteer fax company.

Frijojanan orifice like a bug-eyed lice eater.

The Canadian federal government denied my friend's papers. Billionaire drug- and human-trafficking entrepreneurs are what H.S government want.

hm. hm.

WHICH INTERESTS ARE BEING MOBILIZED AND SERVED BY THIS AND
WHICH ARE NOT?

That's not the State's idea of friendship. The State's idea preserves
happiness in all its fuzziness – in institutions. CAFE vitrine. The idea
has me harrumph what's the point? A WASP reads a loss of social
status.

I choose to watch television rather than sit through my wife's
schizophrenic channelling. I choose to have one less decision to make.

Advancing the rights of women and girls is as much an issue of national
security as it is an issue of ethics and fairness.

This is a Zone of Tolerance, please settle down. Please listen to me.
For health purposes, please have a BMI between 19 and 23. Please
don't share any tokens; sharing is not accounted for in the budget.
Please maintain the minimum standards. Please do respond to
the questionnaire. Please remit all taxes to me. Please trust me to
understand H.S concerns and to act with H.S best interests at heart.

mm-hm.

WHAT ARE UNSEXY? WHAT ARE NORMALIZED AND WHAT ARE PATHOLOGIZED?

I was told most women will have choked back H.S sperm. I took off my clothes because I was told to. I was a good girl boy.

Noticed H.S grief woman smile wryly. I have to make friends. Like I said, I was a good girl boy.

The confusion of war is such that casualties are inseparable from friendly fire. A rattle. The opposite of home.

H.S never has to go home if there are no borders to cross. Cross-dressing boundaries that is.

If I post these, should I credit them to H.S?

Love does not die a natural death. I will have smothered H.S with a pillow just to show him how much.

oh.

Mono oscillatory begets cum ply vaccination kisses. Parched lips kiss me. The privilege of mobility does not mean I will ever be outside of plastic waters and leftovers i.e., boozy monster.

I love H.S throat chakra. A gulp flash forward. We (I + H.S) dwell in bodies. Friend and enemy. There is always three, my darling beard.

I will have written "humiliate" to describe H.S deranged ladies.

Ally cats move through walls.

H.S, so to speak, invented the social contradictions that make my freedom necessary.

Is it not fully furnished? It's never finished.

I made things and time erases all the vestiges of myself.

On the pretext that H.S does not exist; that it means nothing ...

I think that the germ of every question contains its answer – both in an absolute and a conceptual way. Questioning we can't get away from ... But maybe there's something about the interrogation that's dispensable. Why do I question? If I can't accept questioning as a mode of being, what do I have? What, through questioning, am I attempting to form?

hm. hm.

Unless something extraordinary happens. Chronic obstruction. Pulmonary disease. A history of ends.

I should try political activism sometime. Being around me is a relief.

Pacific Standard daytime hour (GMT–8). The Western Front. The radial symmetry. The certain manifold. The sense of impending doom. What a difference the night makes.

Something extraordinary better happen soon. H.S demands, "remove your government, they don't care about you."

I should try to forget the difference between difference and difference.

H.S shows me an image of an orange rectangular block pile.

Oh. I don't understand architecture. Illuminata narrativas circumscribe a grand ole id party.

oh.
oh.
oh.

Army forces say "cranium" or "skull" instead of "head." Refer to "Iraqis" as "the bad guys." "Go-pills" hard to swallow not "dextroamphetamine" gulp down. Attention to whether the blind spot consists of "friendly forces" not "allied forces." I am not "anti-Israeli" I am "pro human rights." Servers seat "guests" instead of "patrons" at a two-top. Buy into stocks and bonds as a "partner," never an "employee." Go out for a boozy brunch and share intimate secrets as "friends" not "colleagues." These aren't "glasses" they're "jars." "Sexy" instead of "interesting" in regard to that line of poetry. "He packs wool sheared in April, honey" and "sells potatoes" not "The Body Shop" and "Eddie Bauer." "Warriors of Society" in place of "police" and "security forces." In place of "187." "Suicide by cop" and "who strikes and consoles, consoles and strikes?" I can't be your "husband" when I'm such an "asshole." Was it in fact "rape" or did you just have "a bad time?" My "heart" is tumultuous like an Instagram "like." Calling out urban corridor as "friends" not "comrades." Can I come to the party? I'm "queer" too! Exchange "Gonk" not "Afghani" currency. Heartfelt disclosure of the "casualization of labour" meets offhand disregard for the "precaritization of labour." Routine moments where we can "debrief," never "vent," and hold ourselves unaccountable. We need more business perspectives, because the profession is mostly run by "white women." "You're so hot, I'm, like, in love with you." I didn't realize "orgasm constraints" were in the "Republic." I'm not "a misogynist"; I'm just suffering from "awkward masculinity." Reply All to a "letter of contemplation," shred a "pink slip." This is the present-day function of the expression "the class struggle," discreetly re-baptized the "social question." How about referring to "play money." when basked in "economic capital." Sir Wilfrid Laurier looks like "Spock" and smells like "maple syrup" if you rub his face just right. Say "intervention" then say "complicity." "Apologized" then "displaced." Vancouver city councillors deny "gentrification" is "genocide." Somehow mental health "workers" align themselves with "management." "Commoners" are "settlers." It used to be called a "labour of love." Negri and Hardt have discovered "affection." When "poetry" becomes a "process-related" McGuffin. "Don't kill yourself" after you "settle down."

Some people don't know the shtick! Canned HEAT laughter in the background. Don't know the shtick! Some people get to sip COFFEE all day long and all night! Some people are fired from their job because they left a single COFFEE bean on the CAFE floor. Some orders are clearer than others. Some orders are more opaque than others. Some friends are better than others. Some foes are better than others. Some friends are foes, some foes friends. Some friends just need a good liking. Canned HEAT laughter in the background! Some orders are mistakes and some mistakes are orders. Some people with degrees work in COFFEE shops to make a living. Some COFFEE makers are convinced making COFFEE is outside of their experience. Some people think this is not my life! Some people buy a gun post-haste pink slip. Canned HEAT laughter in the background! Some rebellions are followed by a period of oppression. Some oppression breeds resistance. Some Mondays are hump days! Some people never get to work. Some work is not available for everybody. Some work is invisible. Some work requires a body and other bodies. Some of the parts are greater than the whole. Some times it is already too late.

My daddy and I shared thoughts and respect for soldiers suffering from PTSD.

I agreed the travesties of war are far from comprehendible. I agreed there is documentation of soldiers raping wives' beauty sleep. I agreed the travesties of war are far from comprehendible. I agreed pharmaceutical testing on soldiers produced consequential shifts in dopamine levels.

Wives reported their husbands acted like "Neanderthals" and society responded with a swift "Stop complaining, Wives!" and "Finally you're getting some, Husbands!"

Sixties sexual revolution only started because the State's conditions were perfect.

Witches spit fair game sex workers. Further scrutinized in recent media headlines for casting liberty spells under the name Feminism.

I agreed with him on a lot of matters. I could talk to him. My daddy and I will have sipped green tea dipped in burnt toast.

But my daddy, like all good boomers, advises me not to dwell on the negative and think positively.

Always look on the Brightside. Don't grumble, give a whistle.

I agreed I am what I feel.

oh.

Hip Mason jar filled with cash placed on kitchen linoleum. Destination wedding invite is circulated on Facebook to all my friends. A white wedding. A resurrection of H.S diseased alcoholic father.

Perform a horizontal friendliness with a specific origin myth. Heterosex fantasies. The joys of mortgage sex. Besmirched garments ripe for plucking. Dribble and froth surface the sea. I was offered a knife with which to stab H.S.

Designer crossbreeding is expensive. COFFEE in the morning with H.S wife is a terrifying apparition. Separates H.S from duty and the influence of accident.

I drive up to Fort St. James for fifteen hours in utter darkness with two friends. A moose's alien ass trots out from the bushel. Bulbous oblong shape and a bellow demand me to drive confidently. Handle with care. The asphalt shone.

Because I knew I would find my way there.

a-ha.

On the pretext female friends do not exist. That it means nothing.

"On the one hand fraternal friendship appears alien to the public realm, but on the other hand traditional philosophical discourse has tied the friend-brother to virtue, to justice, and to moral and political reason."

"The relationship – developed in private – to the singularity and heterogeneity of the other qua other involves the law and thus [H.S] universality and homogeneity, i.e., [H.S] public life as citizen."

I invent the social contradictions that make H.S freedom necessary.

yeah.

FORGET POETRY

Without all the benefits of caffeine, I preview new security measures with a bone at my hip.

Forget about defending why I refuse my former workplace as source material. Academicized hoopla over frightening lack of Insite.

Move to a new city for a new job to make new friends.

Forget the perfect place to watch the world go by. Forget about sabbatical. Forget about ninety-nine problems, *The Red Album*. Forget about starting the New Year with more poetry. Forget to begin H.S reading with an acknowledgement of territory. Sorry, complaints again. Forget about plastic pastoral petunias. Forget the coke-addled neon signs of gravity and grace.

Forget to disclose personal plot points to strangers and friends. H.S wonders why I hang out with poets. The poets only publish me because H.S so pretty.

H.S vulnerabilities are used against him by lady poets.

nah.

Freond of toady *freogan* adores and deprives lingua franca. *Frændi* destroyed the dead notes and the semblance of security.

In August, the leaves cringe. Mourn bloom beauty. H.S complains he don't live in no democracy. There is lots of time in the bright day CAFE to ponder what went wrong between old and new. A vitrine encases customers like quotation marks.

I want to know how H.S utilizes his time off. *Freond* hyphen fire. All time all the time. Leisure. Reassure me.

If I'm an optimist …

a-ha.

No investigation. No education. Cavalierly dismiss all authentic concerns for identity politics. Predisposed to do X or feel Y. Never squirt down, never face down, squirt. The human body has no need for canned cow.

A friendship goes beyond the proximity of the con-generic double. Beyond fraternity, and yet brings with it the genetic connection of fraternity.

H.S best friend is the one who not only wishes him well, but wishes it for H.S own sake.

A man is his own best friend. Therefore he ought to love himself best.

I wish to believe in each other because I want, in vain, to believe in myself.

hm. hm.

I am going to go home and read Nietzsche and determine whether females are capable of theorizing and organizing and making friends.

Species boredom. Unhorse *Ungestalt* to the Herculean wolves.

The feeling is unfounded. Not in the object. Not in the subject. Pulls out, now skip a beat. *Tais-toi!*

My best friend is also my best enemy, and my best enemy is also my best friend. My antithesis is someone to be truly admired. H.S a real bitch.

Emotional Needs Assessment detects it is not a lack of love, but a lack of friendship that makes unhappy marriages.

mm. mm.

I am getting off the plane and transferring to a domestic flight.

A New World Trade Center riddled with protective perforations.
No need to bomb this majestic building, Vito Acconci has done
the job for you. Lucerne tunnels from one side to the next. A space
for people to go outside of habit.

Suggests it's an amalgamation of individualism and collectivism
coming to a head. Transfer corridors separate people. But there is
comfort, at times, in isolation. Perhaps there are no possibilities
for people in space.

Governments maintain the patina of reconciliation. It is in the
embankment between tar fields when limitations ascribed by ethical
standards turn multiples into a killer, a psychopath, a depressive.

A perfect pairing. Amuse Bush. Inside and outside only matters when
meta turns ontological.

And I do love surfaces if you can push them, if you can bulge them,
if you can do activities with them.

When buildings are no longer monuments.

oh.

The one with all the women out there who hate women. Who've been lied to by their menses.

The one where H.S says even the position of "fuck other women, i'm just going to deal with men to get what i need" is in reality a position of relation to other women.

The one where I fight the temptation to indulge in yearning for actual appearances. Fantasy also wards off the threat of outside invasions and unstable sexualities.

The one where I am a perfectly good friend who might not be a perfectly moral one.

The one with the line between fighting and conflict.

The one where H.S palaces will topple, even Atlas. Over H.S cities grass will grow.

The one with my feminist nemesis.

"The one where my trust has been violated. The red walls on which the images hang are an inner sanctuary where transgression is sanctioned. Violation is a transgression. Betrayal can make a boundary where there has been none."

The one with the recording.

The one where H.S thinks it is a little presumptuous or prescriptive to concern oneself with people's actions or politics outside the group. The one where H.S reminds that the purpose of the group is for "community," "empathy," and a "safe space" where learning can happen.

The one where H.S anxiety buffs Miss Ogyny.

The one with the space for H.S to talk about H.S whiteness.

The one where I am self-righteous over and under the influence.

The one where I make a unique weaponized suit of iron and H.S feels unsafe.

most Artforum readers will have sex with me
swapping art with friends in the past
it was casual
now pieces are worth so much more
I have to be more scrupulous
hot HEAT distrust   mobs of women
sun HEAT on the back of my calves
feonds ou trolls
the oil-baron daughter thinks Bartleby
will have lived past excess
jerk off like the Peter Gabriel era
appropriation of African music
most of the artworks I have are mementos of friendship
but they aren't necessarily the best work
of the people concerned
most of these networks tell me what to do
when all I want is serious sincerity
my hot oily cunt buys a drink at the Fairmont
I reinvent love   erudite jaw spasm
a sway and hip-joint tug
more and more in isolation
will H.S be more bored the kinder I am to him?

forces remain indistinguishable from the
Marines and Army
& push corpus past limits
all impossible the more
police and security
are married
///
je vais death drive to the sea
multiples of twice all exponential
labour loves labour
xenia loves *xenia*
///
some people say McDonald's is gangsta
some people like to play Who Wants to Be a Liberal
some people ask their doctors if the Welfare Food Challenge is safe
some people stopped eating meat and started
sucking back Happy Planets
///
ridejoykilldrawninhalves
ampersand

titled turkey neck
exposes my vulnerable protagonist
faultline exposure vile seethes
assignee reprieve
little remains of happiness
much less eloquent reverie
female honour   a damaged nose
immaculate women are
honest business partners
snobby bitches insist on COFFEE
as a mouth replacement
serves as media
code or semiotic system
H.S back tattoo scrawled in Ye Olde script
social capital fracture
a tame wolf   a magic spell
he bites my honker in public
reduce   voice to sexy   baby   maybe
ay   an impasse
am I saying friendly fire is everywhere?
nay   yay

///
what colour is it?
everywhere
inoculate the enemy inside
outside enemy
///
my friend tells me:
"I am not the enemy"
///
I don't feel bad about people I killed
what's worse than wheeling out the driveway
crossing picket
lines?
///
the logical constituency
soldiery social-path
econo Mickey and Mini Cooper
people who fight wars
have more in common with
other combatants than the
the people controlling
lines

commune itches
flock   see now   see nihil
a peel cast off
in the restive border-state
unintended errors   intentional cruelty
isn't it a good idea to
become my own master
drink my own milkshake?
the same as brewing COFFEE
I cannot recycle the empty COFFEE bag
this is a high priority for Ethical Bean COFFEE
///
coital dance and piecemeal blow hoards
skip torpor
click click click
clock clock clock
///
indifferent boner. huff n' puff lobelia
idea-ology-a-band-on

pussy pink *polis*
insects separated by dominant hierarchy
librarian bobbed pink ghetto
bonnet macaque feeds on fruits   nuts   seeds   flowers
invertebrates   serials
exist as communally to humans
raid crops and houses
ants   bees
nuptial flights are seasonal
workers are wingless
virgins lay non-inseminated eggs
a worker performs
some sort of a microwave machine
reproduction considered
a cheap *salope*
Dogville colony
Nicole Kidman walks out of the cinema after seeing H.S results
advantage of functional sterility   every worker assumes
the social contract is destroyed   post-coitus blues
Björk Guðmundsdóttir eats H.S costume
colony cohesion dissolves
aggressive behaviour
results in hierarchies
fucking is repressed

entropy fails to measure the number of guesswork
failure in handling the Mauser accordingly
breathe vanish turn-bolt
sometimes a little tyranny gets this party started
H.S image is great when he walks
       fragile   riskier exorcises for butts
NO SENTENCE PLAYED THE ROLE OF MEDIATOR HERE
I swaddle a grenade
H.S has chicken cunt all over H.S body
meme genera shares a voice other than doubt
It's my time to shine BRITISH COLUMBIA!
PEE HARDER is the minstrel amount of labour
propaganda water breaker pusher kan da har
I want to da har

'twas a tome weld by Clotho's thimble
flower bloom at my bare feels
woven into obese dreams bout property
de(numb)erable nature
if I find value through feeling, what does a banker feel?
next time I will address
how urban planning isn't home anymore
how *malakismenos* is characterized as unmistakably feminized
how *désabritement* is a French translation of *aletheia*
how a decapitalized friendship moulds   pupates
true freedom will always lie in the ability to make friends?
fuck a fake friend where your real friends at?
on the toe beat throat crease
I work so hard   and   still   nobody cares
and I shouldn't either!
I choose who to lie with but don't be fooled
H.S put no ring on it, the target of the crime
pop go pills   start treating me
but stop calling me friend
do not call me friend

The impossibility of "fellow feeling" is itself the confirmation of injury. The call of such pain, as a pain that cannot be shared through empathy, is a call not just for an attentive hearing, but also for a different kind of inhabitance. It is a call for action, and a demand for collective politics, as a politics based not on the possibility that we might be reconciled, but on learning to live with the impossibility of reconciliation, or learning that we live with and beside each other, and yet we are not as one.

—SARA AHMED

"White," "hard," and "hot" are certainly predicative terms; but is it possible to say that "friend" defines, in this sense, a coherent class? Strange as it may seem, "friend" shares this characteristic with another species of non-predicative terms: insults.

—GIORGIO AGAMBEN

You don't have what it takes to be my nemesis.

—CACONRAD

NOTES

ASK NOT WHAT YOUR FRIENDS CAN DO FOR YOU BUT WHAT YOU CAN DO FOR YOUR FRIENDS (2)

Quotes from Paul Boyce and statistics on "friendly fire" deaths were sourced from the article "Is the Army Lying About Friendly Fire Deaths?" by Mark Benjamin on *Salon* online.

SOON AFTER, I STARTED SPITTING ON MY FRIENDS (6)

Ulrike Meinhof's daughter, Bettina Röhl, writes a scathing personal attack of her mother's life as a radical Marxist and co-founder of the Red Army Faction (RAF) in *So macht Kommunismus Spass* (translated as *This Is How Communism Is Fun*, published in 2006). Röhl is the antithesis of her mother and is often portrayed as seeking revenge against her in the media for destroying her childhood, and yet at times is treated by foreign officials as though she is Meinhof reincarnated, living vicariously through a phantom. She writes: "I'm capable of separating the personal and professional, but all anyone wants to say is: 'you can't trust her motivation because she's the terrorist's daughter'" (quoted by Kate Connolly in *The Guardian* online). *The personal is professional, the professional is personal.* Let it be clear to the reader: the relationship between mothers and daughters falls short of friendly fire – because there is nothing friendly between mothers and daughters – there is mostly love.

RED BELLS STILL HANG ON MANY DOORS (8)

The itemization of Harry Schmidt's financial losses as well as the charges laid against him were found and collated in Eileen Flynn's *How Just Is the War on Terror? A Question of Morality.*

"HEAT" is a military acronym that stands for "High-Explosive Anti-Tank."

RIGHT-TO-MASTURBATE-AT-WORK (10)

Many of the lines in this poem are collaged from three survivors of the Tarnak Farm Incident in 2002 when U.S. Air Force Pilot, Harry Schmidt, dropped a 500-pound laser bomb on Canadian troops in Kandahar, Afghanistan. The survivors reveal how "military life was key to their recovery" (quoted by Mary Ormsby in *The Star*), refusing to leave Canada's military-industrial complex as it provided for them what they loved most of all.

I HATE THIS CONJUGATION TOO, BUT IN FRENCH IT'S CALLED THE "FUTURE ANTERIOR" WHEREBY THE PAST AND THE FUTURE ARE INEXTRICABLY LINKED TO TRAUMA (11)

"criming" is a Dorothy Trujillo Lusk coinage.

I AM ROLLING IN SELF-DEFENCE (13)

For Harry Schmidt's side of the story see "Harry Schmidt's War" by Bryan Smith in *Chicago* mag online.

I SPEAK AS H.S FOR THE FIRST AND FINAL TIME (15)

COFFEE 5-2 was a call sign for an F-16 fighter aircraft flown by Harry Schmidt, drawn from an article by Chesapeake in the *National Review*. A call sign is a unique identifier monitored and communicated by military units during wartime. Call signs are routinely changed, as surveilling enemy intelligence is a routine tactic.

SOCIETY OF THE RECEPTACLE (16)

The term "dirty war" has variegated significations. As a proper name it connotes a period of state terrorism in Argentina where political dissidents were hunted down and "disappeared." "Clean" and "dirty" wars are also racialized terms, as the former tends to signify war between whites (i.e., WWI and WWII) where the latter involves people of colour (i.e., the Gulf War).

IFF THE CONDITIONS ARE PERFECT (17)

"IFF" stands for "Identification, friend or foe."

OFFICIAL PINK SLIP (18)

"Operation Enduring Freedom" is the official name used by the government of the United States to describe operations in Afghanistan from October 2001 to December 2014.

naive leviathan. Not all-heal bender chemist (22)

"coxcomb red" is borrowed from a song title of the same name by Ohia, from the album *Ohia: Songs*.

"*Mercury is the* Internet." In the cold box office of the Western Front, Ariana Reines and I sat closely while she performed an interpretation of an Internet printout of my astrological chart. Danielle LaFrance. May 8, 1983. 08:00:00 AM PDT. Burnaby, CAN. The time is not exact. Rather than requesting this information from Marcellin Jean-Joseph LaFrance, I should have asked the source herself, Valerie Jay Megaw (née Baby B.). At some point during this session, Reines said to me: "Mercury is the Internet," the planet of communication. I will not forget how her long acrylics circled a loop. In order to overcome my writer's block I needed the words to exit from my root chakra, my cunt, then to my mouth, and back again. The origin of the word, unbounded energy, unmediated id – the pathway to writing was to be found somewhere on the border of the sentence and bodily desire.

And while this experience with Reines left an impression, it took me a few days to look at that Internet printout and remember my birthday is not May 8, 1983.

when the planets align in opposition (26)
"OTI" stands for "on the Internet," in contrast to "IRL," "in real life."

when H.S around the anarchists (28)
"*how the strong will survive / at the end of their gun*" is a lyric from the 1985 single, "We Run," by Canadian New Wave band Strange Advance. Thank you, Ian Cameron and Drew Arnott, for granting permission to include these lyrics as lines of poetry. If only you knew how frequently this song plays at my house. Now you both know.

THE ONE WHERE THE GANG GETS BACK TOGETHER (35)
Direct quotations in this poem are sourced from Nietzsche's *Human, All Too Human*.

THE ONE WHERE AFTER THE RED WEDDING H.S IS SOMEONE I CAN NO LONGER BE FRIENDS WITH (36)
Direct quotations in this poem are sourced from Sandra Lynch in her essay "Aristotle and Derrida on Friendship."

There is much contention surrounding the translation of the Aristotelean line, *o philoi, oudeis philos* (o friends, there are no friends). In his essay "Friendship," Giorgio Agamben historicizes the error of translation, from Montaigne to Nietzsche, and finally to the great post-structuralist himself, Derrida. The line in question actually reads as such: *oi* (omega with subscript iota) *philio, oeudeis philos*; he who has (many) friends, has no friends. Considering Derrida's entire conceit for the *The Politics of Friendship* was established around the former motto, Agamben expresses his dismay towards the error: "I was astonished, when [Derrida's] book was published ... not to find any trace of the problem. If the motto – apocryphal according to modern philologists – appeared there in its original form, it was certainly not out of forgetfulness" but was "the essential motto to the book's strategy."

H.S just lays around as Red Mars slowly teeters Earth (41)

This poem was largely drawn from Kim Stanley Robinson's sci-fi novel *Red Mars*. Arthur C. Clarke blurbs the front cover: "The best novel on the colonization of Mars that has ever been written. It should be required reading for the colonists of the next century."

them Benevolent Beasts and Jesus Punk Misogynists (53)

"*Dick.*" It's interesting to note how Amazon has recently pilot ordered Kraus's infamous book *I Love Dick*. The representation of lived life as a multi-scaled project that traverses female abjection, conceptual fucking, obsession, high theory, and art banter will register quite differently as a streamed story.

murder trigger animals (56)

From: DANIELLE LAFRANCE
Date: Sunday, 6 April, 2014 10:17 AM
To: Roger Farr
Subject: Re: Nietszche's whip

As long as she obeys out of total love that is ;)

Thursday?

On 5 April 2014 13:03, Roger Farr wrote:

That's Salome in the carriage......gives some new signification to the line "You go to women? Do not forget the whip!"

It's not for the woman! :-)

(killer bees) (killer friends) (57)

"Στην υγειά σας!" is Greek for "Cheers."

REPRODUCTIVE LABOUR IS REDUCED THANKS TO THE REMOVAL OF CLP (61)

"CLP" is a registered one-step solution, which stands for "Cleaner, Lubricant and Preservative" and is used to protect firearms from corrosion. For what it's worth, C.L.P. also stands for the Communist Labour Party.

"KIA" or "Killed in Action" is a casualty classification.

WHATEVER DID HAPPEN TO FREDDY DEMUTH? (65)

Italicized text can be found in ryan fitzpatrick's chapbook *dealingwithit. gif* and has been used with permission.

all H.S friends really know how to liberate (70)

"*Cute Compactus Est*" borrows from the *Narrative of the Life of James Allen*, alias Jonas Pierce, alias James H. York, alias Burley Grove, the Highwayman: Being His Death-bed Confession, to the Warden of the Massachusetts State Prison, an autobiographical confession authored by James Allen, bound and clothed in his own skin. The front cover is decorated with the label "HIC LIBER WALTONIS CUTE COMPACTUS EST"; Walton being yet another alias the author and prisoner went by.

H.S throat was cut out (72)

Sometime around the London riots in 2011 Louis Cabri shared a video with comrades and myself. In the video ("Ibrahim Kashoush (ابراهيم قاشوش) le chanteur de la révolution") protestors swarm Hama in central Syria, mourning and crying out for the poet Ibrahim Qashoush who was brutally murdered on July 4, 2011, found in the Orontes River with his throat cut and his vocal cords removed by Bashar al-Assad's militias. The protest chant, or "call and response," "Yalla Erhal Ya Bashar," or "Come on, Bashar, time to leave," was attributed to Qashoush. Moving in coordination through the urban corridors, the group responds "sympathetically" to the call with chanting or bodily movements.

I routinely transfer (74)

The word "dethe" is from an image of the Death Bell from Richard Rolle's manuscript, roughly from the third quarter of the fifteenth century. The viewer's relationship to this image would have been private. The image encompasses both the written word and the visual image, but is also connected to sound. The words surround the bell held by the skeleton, or Death, become larger and larger, as they navigate towards the edges of the blue frame. Such attention reminds us of the intimate nature of Death and finitude. Kristeva notes how such close proximity is a crucial moment: "it is a vision that opens out not on but on endurance." There are different ways to hold attention, one through looking, and another through listening. Acute attention. With attention comes a form of self-discipline and affective training. To hear Death? The word, again, is "dethe"; can't you see it, hear it? How do we hear our own death? Like the death-bell image, it sounds, it sounds. Only we can hear it when it comes. The text is telling us something, but it is the size of the text, reminding us of a concrete poem, of an image. The visual sound reaches forth like a crude skeletal, yet muscular, finger aligning us with rotting flesh, the word/the image now unbound from logic. For me, it evokes the line from Freud: "We have shown an unmistakable tendency to put death aside, to eliminate it from life." In these old manuscripts death is very much present, it is a reminder that we will die.

The state of tongues is a warning to mouths, just as the violence of the State, like death, slowly advances. Qashoush's murder is a reminder of poetry that resounds, that makes something happen.

THAT SNIFFER DOG HAS BEEN UP MY ASS ALL MY LIFE! (79)

"THAT SNIFFER DOG..." was bellowed at city councillors on the Downtown Eastside Local Area Plan after three days of public hearings in March 2014. See *The Mainlander* for a discussion on the DTES dispersal plan.

WHICH INTERESTS ARE BEING MOBILIZED AND SERVED BY THIS AND WHICH ARE NOT? (80)

This poem was written in collaboration with Patrick Morrison.

"CAFE" is a military acronym that stands for Communications Automation Follow-On Effort.

POETRY HIDES A TRUTH ABOUT FRIENDLY FIRE (83)

"*the germ of every question* ... " is from an email sent to me by Patrick Morrison during my stay in Malamata, Greece.

THE ONE WHERE FRIENDLY FIRE IS REDUCED TO SOCIAL SLIGHTS (84)

"You people will never be safe. Remove your government, they don't care about you" was spoken by Michael Adebolajo after killing a soldier in the Woolwich district of London on May 22, 2013 (quoted in Berardi).

THERE IS NO POINT SEARCHING FOR NEW LANGUAGE (85)

"This is the present-day function of the expression 'the class struggle,' discreetly re-baptized 'the social question'" is from Christine Delphy's *Separate and Dominate: Feminism and Racism after the War on Terror.*

"It used to be called a 'labour of love.' Negri and Hardt instead have discovered 'affection,'" is drawn from Silvia Federici.

MY DADDY WAS MY BEST FRIEND (87)

"Post-traumatic stress disorder (PTSD) is estimated to afflict upwards of 30 percent of veterans, and while resources have been added, treatment for psychological ailments is sorely lacking. The greatest threat by far posed by traumatized veterans is not to others, but to themselves: it is estimated that 22 veterans in the U.S. are committing suicide every day" (Kennard quoted in Bifo's *Heroes: Mass Murder and Suicide*).

"Brightside": My daddy wants "Always Look on the Bright Side of Life," by Monty Python's Eric Idle, to be played during his funeral.

SORORI-TITTIES (89)

Text in quotes is from the *Politics of Friendship* by Jacques Derrida.

H.S WILL HAVE STABBED ME IN MARSEILLES (94)

When I travelled to Marseilles in 2014, a man began to stalk me.

> From: [Name redacted]
> Date: July 23, 2014 at 8:59:52 AM GMT+2
> To: DANIELLE LAFRANCE
> Subject: Re: COUCOU DANIELLE CA VA ?
>
> TAKE YOUR ORGUEIL AND EAT IT OR that your orgueil eat it it up to you.
>
> I dont need to received lessons ALMOST FROM A GIRL LIKE YOU.
>
> TAKE YOUR LESSONS AND YOUR ADVICE FOR GREECE GIRL THAT YOU ARE NOT FOR ME.
>
> I PREFER THE TRUE YOGOURT FROM BULGARIA your copie :)
>
> STRANGE,YES YOU ARE STRANGE SUREEEEEEEEEEEEEEEEE.
>
> I PREFER PEOPLE NORMAL than girls who have nothing like you.
>
> Stay to your countrie where you leave or to YOU COUNTRIE WHERE ARE FROM , yes your countrie where people HAS SPEND ALL HEIR TIME TO LIE TO EVERYBODY, YOUR COUNTRIE WHERE PEOPLE WHO WORK ON CHURCHS HAS MORE MONEY THAN PEOPLE WHO LEAVE IN GREACE.
>
> I DONT LIKE PEOPLE WHO LIE AND or PEOPLE WHO STILL people who has nothing for eat.
>
> SO, DO YOUR SALADE GREC FOR SOMEONELSE NEVER TO ME PLEASE BECAUSE I DON T LIKE SALADE GREC I PREFER TRUE SALADE OK ??
>
> SO go somewhere else if i am ok and let me be please.
>
> HAVE A NICE RETURN TO YOUR countrie where you leave and, DON t FORGET YOUR BOOK or YOUR JOURNAL OK ?
>
> ;)
>
> BYE

THE ONE WHERE I HATE H.S SO MUCH RIGHT NOW (95)

"Your palaces will topple. Even Atlas," is from Ovid's *Metamorphoses*, specifically the "Flood" section.

Direct quotations are sourced from Bell Hooks. In *Art on My Mind: Visual Politics*, Hooks describes how photographer Lyle Ashton Harris displayed her nude image without her consent at a vernissage in SOHO. These images, taken of her while asleep, assume intimacy and trust between Harris and Hooks – a friendship. When we take from people it does not necessarily mean they want to be our friends.

pussy pink *polis* (104)

"some sort of a microwave machine" is a line included in a report (quoted in Berardi) concerning the complaints of Aaron Alexis, a thirty-four-year-old U.S. veteran who opened fire performing a mass shooting at the Washington Navy Yard on September 16, 2013.

entropy fails to measure the number of guesswork (105)

The line "It's my time to shine BRITISH COLUMBIA!" is from the song "It's Our Time to Shine," sung during Expo '86 by an ensemble of performers that included my father Marcellin Jean-Joseph LaFrance, Nancy Nash, Jane Mortifee, and Andy Thomas.

'twas a tome weld by Clotho's thimble (106)

"*malakismenos*" is Greek slang for a top wanker, in the feminine.

The statement "true freedom will always lie in the ability to make friends" is found in Chris Nealon's poem *The Dial*, turned into a question for this poem.

SELECTED SOURCES

Benjamin, Mark. "Is the Army Lying About Friendly Fire Deaths?" *Salon.com*, January 15, 2009.

Berardi, Franco "Bifo." *Heroes: Mass Murder and Suicide.* New York: Verso, 2013.

Chesapeake. "The friendly-fire trial." *NationalReview.com*, January 23, 2003.

Connolly, Kate. "Child of the revolution returns to haunt Fischer." *TheGuardian.com*, January 27, 2001.

Delphy, Christine. *Separate and Dominate: Feminism and Racism after the War on Terror.* Trans. David Broder. London: Verso, 2015.

Derrida, Jacques. *Politics of Friendship.* Trans. George Collins. London: Verso, 1997.

Federici, Silvia. *Revolution at Point Zero: Housework, Reproduction, and Feminist Struggle.* Oakland: PM Press, 2012.

fitzpatrick, ryan. *dealingwithit.gif* Vancouver: Publication Studio, 2016.

Flynn, Eileen P. *How Just Is the War on Terror? A Question of Morality.* New York: Paulist, 2007.

Freud, Sigmund. "Thoughts for the Times on War and Death." Trans. James Strachey. *panarchy.org*, 2000–.

Hooks, Bell. *Art on My Mind: Visual Politics.* New York: The New Press, 1995.

Kennard, Matt. "How the 'War on Terror' Came Home," *TheGuardian.com*, accessed 17 September 2013, qtd. in Berardi, *Heroes: Mass Murder and Suicide.*

Kraus, Chris. *I Love Dick.* Los Angeles: Semiotext(e), 2006.

Kristeva, Julia. *Black Sun: Depression and Melancholia.* New York: Columbia University Press, 1989.

Lynch, Sandra. "Aristotle and Derrida on Friendship." *Contretemps* July 2002: n. pag. *sydney.edu.au/contretemps/index.html*, 2000–.

Nealon, Chris. *The Dial.* Brooklyn: The Song Cave, 2014.

Nietzsche, Friedrich. *Human, All Too Human.* Trans. Faber, Marion and Stephen Lehmann. Lincoln: University of Nebraska Press, 1996.

Ormsby, Mary. "Three Tarnak Farm survivors remember 2002 friendly fire incident." *TheStar.com*, November 10, 2012.

Ovid, *Metamorphoses.* Trans. Henry T. Riley. *Gutenberg.org*

Robinson, Kim Stanley. *Red Mars.* New York: Bantam, 1993.

Smith, Bryan. "Harry Schmidt's War." *Chicagomag.com*, April 2005.

Songs: Ohia. "Coxcomb Red."
The Lioness. Secretly Canadian,
2000. CD.

Strange Advance. "We Run." *2wo*.
Capitol, 1985. LP.

syriancitizens. "Ibrahim Kashoush
(ابرهيم قاشوش) le chanteur
de la révolution." YouTube,
July 10, 2011.

Wallstam, Maria, Tristan Markle,
and Nathan Crompton.
"Downtown Eastside dispersal
plan approved by City Council."
TheMainlander.com, March 17,
2014.

ACKNOWLEDGEMENTS

I will have acknowledged this book was predominantly written on the unceded and ancestral territories of the Musqueam, Skwxwú7mesh Úxwumixw, Stó:lō, and Tsleil-Waututh peoples.

Some of these poems have appeared in some variation in the following publications: Line, About a Bicycle, Dreamboat, Armed Cell, and Tripwire. An earlier version of this book came in the form of a chapbook Pink Slip, published by Standard Ink & Copy Press in 2013. Pink Slip was performed along with images from my personal archive during my residency at the John Snow House, Calgary, in 2013.

Many friends and foes helped me realize this book. I am mostly indebted to the former for their critical attention, invaluable assistance, and emotional support, in no particular order: Patrick Morrison, Andrea Actis, Deanna Fong, Louis Cabri, Megan Hepburn, Anahita Jamali Rad, Kaylin Pearce, Carolyn Richard, Ben Hynes, Nikki Reimer, Milena Varzonovtseva, Rachel Zolf, Jeff Derksen, Holly Chemerika, Alexis Baker, ryan fitzpatrick, Andi Javor, Lisa Robertson, Shazia Hafiz Ramji, Fred Wah, Michael Barnholden, Rachel Baumann, Alex Muir, Dina González Mascaró, Joelle Ciona, Stacey Ho, Adrienne Connelly, Emily Fedoruk, Honey, Robin Simpson, Melissa Guzman, almost everyone involved in 2013's In(ter)ventions Residency at the Banff Centre, CAConrad, Steven Tong, Cecily Nicholson, Donato Mancini, Natalie Knight, David Buuck, Dorothy Trujillo Lusk, Roger Farr, Mercedes Eng, Aaron Vidaver, Reg Johanson, Shawna Delgaty, Anna Ruddick, all of the self-identified women who comprised About a Bicycle, Matthew Fehr, and, always, my sister, Jeunesse LaFrance. Many thanks also go to my mom, dad, stepmom, and stepsister.

I will have also remembered Malamata, the tiny Greek village, where this book was mostly resuscitated.

I will have returned to the Balkans two years later, this time to Sofia, Bulgaria, where this book smothered the other side of those seemingly old preoccupations with friendship and total war.

Danielle LaFrance is a poet, occasional librarian, and independent scholar. She is the author of *Species Branding* (CUE, 2010) and the chapbook *Pink Slip* (SIC, 2013). Between 2012 and 2016, she co-organized the feminist materialist collective and journal series *About a Bicycle*, with Anahita Jamali Rad. Her work deals with the ways "total war" and "Empire" infiltrate social relations as well as the intersections between language, revolutionary action, and self-abolition. And total love. Since 1983 she has mostly resided on the unceded territories of the Musqueam, Skwxwú7mesh Úxwumixw, Stó:lō, and Tsleil-Waututh peoples.

Photo: Melissa Dex Guzman